£20.99

D1635646

Institute of Leadership
& Management

superseries

Managing
Creativity and
Innovation in
the Workplace

FIFTH EDITION

Published for the
Institute of Leadership & Management

ELSEVIER

AMSTERDAM • BOSTON • HEIDELBERG • LONDON • NEW YORK • OXFORD
PARIS • SAN DIEGO • SAN FRANCISCO • SINGAPORE • SYDNEY • TOKYO
Pergamon Flexible Learning is an imprint of Elsevier

Pergamon
Flexible
Learning

Pergamon Flexible Learning is an imprint of Elsevier
Linacre House, Jordan Hill, Oxford OX2 8DP, UK
30 Corporate Drive, Suite 400, Burlington, MA 01803, USA

First edition 1986
Second edition 1991
Third edition 1997
Fourth edition 2003
Fifth edition 2007

Editor: David Pardey

Based on material in previous editions of this work

The views expressed in this work are those of the authors and do not necessarily reflect those of the Institute of Leadership & Management or of the publisher

Notice
No responsibility is assumed by the publisher for any injury and/or damage to persons or property as a matter of products liability, negligence or otherwise, or from any use or operation of any methods, products, instructions or ideas contained in the material herein

British Library Cataloguing in Publication Data
A catalogue record for this book is available from the British Library

Library of Congress Cataloguing in Publication Data
A catalogue record for this book is available from the Library of Congress

ISBN 978-0-08-046441-1

For information on all Pergamon Flexible Learning publications
visit our website at http://books.elsevier.com

Institute of Leadership & Management
Registered Office
1 Giltspur Street
London
EC1A 9DD
Telephone: 020 7294 2470
www.i-l-m.com
ILM is part of the City & Guilds Groups

Typeset by Charon Tec Ltd (A Macmillan Company), Chennai, India
www.charontec.com
Printed and bound in Great Britain

07 08 09 10 11   10 9 8 7 6 5 4 3 2 1

Working together to grow
libraries in developing countries

www.elsevier.com | www.bookaid.org | www.sabre.org

ELSEVIER   BOOK AID International   Sabre Foundation

Contents

Contents

Series preface

Whether you are a tutor/trainer or studying management development to further your career, Super Series provides an exciting and flexible resource to help you to achieve your goals. The fifth edition is completely new and up-to-date, and has been structured to perfectly match the Institute of Leadership & Management (ILM)'s new unit-based qualifications for first line managers. It also harmonizes with the 2004 national occupational standards in management and leadership, providing an invaluable resource for S/NVQs at Level 3 in Management.

Super Series is equally valuable for anyone tutoring or studying any management programmes at this level, whether leading to a qualification or not. Individual workbooks also support short programmes, which may be recognized by ILM as Endorsed or Development Awards, or provide the ideal way to undertake CPD activities.

For learners, coping with all the pressures of today's world, Super Series offers you the flexibility to study at your own pace to fit around your professional and other commitments. You don't need a PC or to attend classes at a specific time – choose when and where to study to suit yourself! And you will always have the complete workbook as a quick reference just when you need it.

For tutors/trainers, Super Series provides an invaluable guide to what needs to be covered, and in what depth. It also allows learners who miss occasional sessions to 'catch up' by dipping into the series.

Super Series provides unrivalled support for all those involved in first line management and supervision.

Unit specification

Title:	Managing creativity and innovation in the workplace	Unit Ref:	M3.06
Level:	3		
Credit value:	1		

Learning outcomes *The learner* will	Assessment criteria *The learner can (in an organization with which the learner is familiar)*	
1. Understand the importance of creativity and innovation for the organization	1.1	Use a technique to encourage creative ideas amongst team members
	1.2	Explain barriers to creative thinking and resistance to innovation within the team
	1.3	Explain how to gain the commitment of others in moving creative ideas forward
	1.4	Evaluate creative and innovative ideas and make reasoned recommendations to managers and others

Workbook introduction

1 ILM Super Series study links

This workbook addresses the issues of *Managing Creativity and Innovation in the Workplace*. Should you wish to extend your study to other Super Series workbooks covering related or different subject areas, you will find a comprehensive list at the back of this book.

2 Links to ILM qualifications

This workbook relates to the learning outcomes of Unit M3.06 Managing creativity and innovation in the workplace from the ILM Level 3 Award, Certificate and Diploma in First Line Management.

3 Links to S/NVQs in management

This workbook relates to the following Unit of the Management Standards which are used in S/NVQs in Management, as well as a range of other S/NVQs:

C2. Encourage innovation in your area of responsibility

4 Workbook objectives

Creativity and innovation have become much more significant issues for all organizations over the last few years. This is a reflection of the increasingly competitive market that all organizations operate in, whether they are in the private, public or voluntary sector. This innovation has been driven by the increasing rate at which new technologies have appeared, the greater wealth of people in developed countries particularly, and changing social patterns.

People will try out new products and services more readily, and organizations have to improve their processes constantly to meet customer demand and manage their costs. Far too many organizations have seen themselves as impregnable until a new organization arrives and they find themselves struggling.

In this workbook we will look at innovation and its closely related idea, creativity. We will examine how creativity leads into innovation, what you can do to encourage creative ideas and assess your organization's readiness to accept these ideas, and what you need to do to implement them.

4.1 Objectives

By the time you have completed the workbook you should be able to:

- distinguish between creativity and innovation;
- recognize the increasing importance of creativity and innovation in organizational success;
- appreciate some of the different techniques that can help you to lead people through a creative ideas generation process;
- select an appropriate creative approach to developing innovations in your organization;
- implement innovative ideas in your organization.

5 Activity planner

Activities 6 and 7 ask you to look at your organization's approach to R&D. You may want to explore this at work now, so that you can start collecting material as soon as possible.

These and several other Activities may provide the basis of evidence for your S/NVQ portfolio. All Portfolio Activities and the Work-based assignment are signposted with this icon.

Session A
The importance of creativity and innovation

1 Introduction

> 'As the births of all living creatures are, at first, misshapen, so are all innovations.'
>
> Francis Bacon (1625)

The arts are all about creativity. We expect artists, sculptors, musicians, writers and performers to see things in new ways, to present new sounds, images and ideas. We look to businesses at the leading edge of their industry, in communications and information technology-based sectors particularly, to develop innovative products and services.

But what about the rest of us, people who aren't creative artists, who work in more everyday organizations, what has creativity and innovation to do with us? This workbook is all about the nature and role of creativity and innovation and what you can do to encourage it in your organization. We will start, in this first session, by looking at just exactly what creativity and innovation are and why they are important for every organization. We'll also look at the implications if organizations don't encourage creativity and innovation in their products and services and in the processes by which these are produced or supplied.

2 What are creativity and innovation?

Let's start by thinking about both ideas and decide what they are and how they differ.

Activity 1

8 mins

What do you think these two words mean. Think about them and write your thoughts down here.

Creativity is:

_____

_____

Innovation is:

_____

_____

There are plenty of different definitions, but here are two that are probably helpful in thinking about the difference between the two ideas. They were used by Dr William Coyne, who was Senior Vice-President for Research and Development of the 3M Corporation, when he gave the sixth UK Innovation Lecture at the Queen Elizabeth II Conference Centre on the 5th March 1996. He distinguished between creativity and innovation by saying that creativity is 'the thinking of novel and appropriate ideas' whereas innovation is 'the successful implementation of those ideas within an organization'. Another way of thinking about this is that creativity is the new or original idea, but innovation is the process by which that idea is turned into practice.

Activity 2 · 3 mins

Thinking about these definitions, what do you think is more important for an organization, to be able to develop creative ideas or to be innovative and turn creative ideas into practice?

You may have said that they need to be both, and ideally they should be. You may have said that, since creativity comes first, that must be more important. Whilst it's true that, without creative ideas, organizations can't be innovative, it is also true that they don't have to develop creative ideas themselves to put them into practice. Innovative organizations can buy in creative ideas, or copy other people's ideas. However, if they aren't innovative, then all the creative ideas in the world will be useless, because they will lack the ability to turn them into real products or services, or change their processes.

The Centre for Exploitation of Science and Technology (CEST) in a 1995 report called *Bridging the Innovation Gap* define the 'innovation gap' as the gap between vision and reality, between generating the creative idea in the first place and the subsequent analysis to identify the potential of the new idea or process and its implementation, what we have called innovation. In other words, the biggest problem facing organizations is not coming up with creative ideas (although that still needs working on) but the innovation that puts them into practice.

The same report went on to distinguish between two types of technical innovation, between:

■ evolutionary innovation, taking the design of existing practices, products or services a step further away from conventional ways of doing things, which is undertaken on a planned basis, or
■ revolutionary innovation, based on 'serendipity' (an opportunity for innovative practices, products or services occurring) which could which cannot be predicted but which the organization must be alert to and supportive of when the occasion arises.

As we shall see, in Session C, neither will occur if the organization isn't prepared to embrace innovation, however it occurs. However, the organization that isn't prepared to accept evolutionary innovation is far less likely to accept something revolutionary.

3 Why are creativity and innovation so important?

Alexander Graham Bell patented the first telephone in 1876 and two years later the first telephone companies started up in the UK. By 1972 only 42% of households had a telephone, rising to around 93% some 20 years later, and has never gone much above this figure. By comparison, the mobile 'phone was introduced in the late 1970s and today, after only 30 years or so, approaching 90% of households have at least one.

Activity 3

5 mins

Why do you think products like mobile phones have been taken up so rapidly, compared with the much slower growth of landlines?

_____

_____

_____

_____

Obviously mobile phones have many advantages over landlines. They can be used wherever the person is, they offer a much wider range of services (text, video, music, as well as ordinary voice communication) and they are small and easy to carry around. However, it's important not to let the convenience and versatility specific to mobile phones to hide some broader factors that apply to many other areas as well.

3.1 Greater wealth

Firstly, here in the wealthy western world, most people live lives of luxury compared to their grandparents and have much higher disposable incomes (income after all fixed expenditure) to spend on goods and services. This makes them more responsive to new ideas and new ways of behaving, because their basic needs have been satisfied and they still have plenty of money left over. Of course, some items (like housing) have become relatively more expensive, but many others have become relatively cheap, as people's incomes have risen. The ordinary telephone was still regarded as a luxury item in the fifties or sixties, but is now seen by many as a basic necessity, and its cost is relatively low.

The availability of a much larger disposable income has also been accompanied by much busier lifestyles. People haven't used the opportunity offered by greater wealth to reduce their hours of work significantly but have simply fitted more into their lives. The proliferation of new products and services has created new opportunities to be busy, whether it's eating out, going to the gym, having a short break abroad, playing computer games or chatting to people around the world via the Internet.

There is also a political and social aspect to these economic changes. Greater wealth is primarily an economic phenomenon, but it is also a social phenomenon – economic growth leads to social changes, as people can afford to change their lifestyles. Several hundred thousand Britons now own houses abroad as well as in the UK. More and more people live alone. Family sizes in Western Europe are falling below replacement size, so that populations would be shrinking if it weren't for net inward migration (more people immigrating than emigrating).

Politically these changes are also important. A few years ago there was great consternation in the UK when it was announced that Italy had (temporarily) overtaken the UK in the size of its economy. Being the fifth largest economy in the world (after the USA, Japan, Germany and China, based on World Bank ratings of Gross National Income) makes this relatively small island with its medium-sized population (21st largest in 2005) far more significant internationally than it would otherwise be. In negotiations with international partners, in the EU, in the World Trade Organization and at the United Nations, the UK's economic power gives us political clout. However, that economic power depends on the creativity and innovation of UK organizations and the people they employ.

3.2 Greater expectations

Secondly, people expect much more from the goods and services on offer. This higher level of expectation is probably related to the first factor – greater relative wealth makes people more demanding of the goods and services they receive, and far less accepting of inferior products or experiences. They are also more adventurous, more ready to try out new things that their parents or grandparents would be more careful about, and also more ready to throw out older items that still work, to buy something new.

This is illustrated by the diffusion of innovation curve, which shows the willingness of people to accept innovative new products and services. The first diagram shows the six different categories as being more or less equal in size, from *Innovators* (who are always keen to try something new) to *Laggards* (who will hold out from trying something to the last).

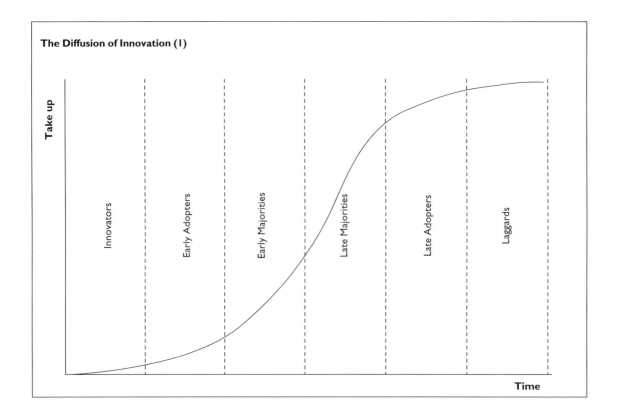

The six different categories shown in the diagram are:

1 *Innovators*, who seek out new products and experiences, and always want to be the first to own new products or try out new services. They will download the Beta versions of new software that still has bugs in it.

2 *Early Adopters*, who respond quickly to new trends but like to wait briefly before trying them out, to iron out the worst problems. These are the people who will buy the first release software.

3 *Early Majorities*, who respond less quickly to trends, waiting for evidence that this is the right purchase decision to make. They will buy the revised first edition (software *v1.1*), which has been changed to take account of the problems Innovators and Early Adopters experienced.

4 *Late Majorities*, who are more resistant to trends but will take them up when they have become widely adopted. They want to buy mainstream products and services that have proved themselves (software *v2.0*).

5 *Late Adopters*, who tend to take up Innovations only when they have become the norm, often after Innovators and even Early Adopters have moved on to something else (software *v3.0*).

6 *Laggards*, who stick with the old ways until they are forced to change, the kind of people who will delight in the 'old ways', who still use typewriters when everyone else is using a computer.

It is quite possible that the curve has got steeper in recent years, that more people are ready to adopt new ideas (*Innovators* and *Early Adopters*) and fewer are *Late Adopters* or *Laggards* (perhaps because the old products or services get withdrawn more quickly). This is shown in the figure below:

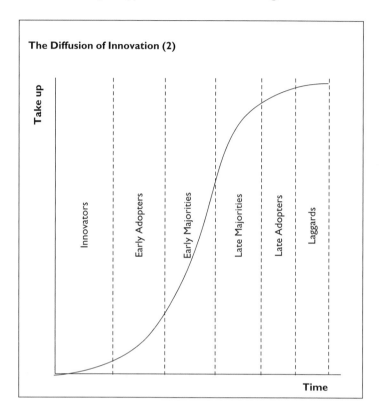

The Diffusion of Innovation (2)

Take up — Innovators — Early Adopters — Early Majorities — Late Majorities — Late Adopters — Laggards — Time

Activity 4

4 mins

Think about your own attitude to innovative products and services, and the behaviour of some other people you know. How would you class yourself and them, in terms of their willingness to try out new products and services?

	Yourself	Person 1	Person 2	Person 3
Innovators				
Early Adopters				
Early Majorities				
Late Majorities				
Late Adopters				
Laggards				

3.3 New products and services

There is a 'chicken and egg' question about the willingness of people to welcome innovative new products and services, and the developments in technology and systems that produce them. If so many new products and services weren't there, would people be so receptive of them? On the other hand, if people weren't so receptive, would there be the incentive to develop them? In reality, there has probably been a parallel development, with the technologies and systems being developed more rapidly as society becomes more willing to try out (and even more demanding of) new products and services, as novelty becomes an end in itself.

4 The importance of R&D

R&D – research and development – lie at the heart of innovative products and services, and depend on the creativity of our scientists, technologists, engineers and product designers, and on the managers who employ and encourage them.

R&D is a very loose term to describe everything from the basic research that goes on in University laboratories to the market testing of new products and services that is organized by market research companies to perfect the shape of a bottle to hold a new drink or the texture of a new biscuit. Often, the link between the one and the other is very long and tenuous. When a research scientist uncovers the curious properties of certain fluoro-carbons (compounds of fluoride and carbon), it is a long route (via the coatings on rockets to reduce friction during launch) to easy-to-clean kitchen utensils.

Case study

A few years ago a PhD student was discussing his research activity. He was investigating the properties of certain artificial (i.e. not naturally occurring) materials for their potential to be used to replace natural muscle in people suffering from certain muscle-wasting diseases. These materials are categorized by their responsiveness to weak electrical signals. These cause the material to stretch or shrink, in the same way that muscles stretch or shrink when they receive weak electrical signals from the brain.

After two years' research, with another year left to complete his research and write his thesis, he had found that the materials he was investigating had very limited potential. They were unlikely to be able to be developed further to be of practical use. Other researchers, looking at other classes of materials, had more success. It was unlikely that his research would lead to any useful products.

Activity 5

3 mins

What can you conclude about the usefulness of his research? Was it worth-while? Why do you think that?

_____

_____

_____

This research didn't lead to any worthwhile products, but what it did do was to narrow down the options for future research, by excluding the class of materials that he had been studying. Much of the research undertaken by pharmaceutical companies falls into this category. There are far more dead-ends than miracle breakthroughs, but the miracle breakthroughs result from many years of painstaking research, much of which produces nothing other than the knowledge that this isn't the way to solve the problem.

The Dyson vacuum cleaner was the result of some 2,000 prototypes, until the right product was developed. In the speech referred to earlier, Bill Coyne reckoned that it took 1,000 new product ideas to produce one successful product in the market. If all this sounds wasteful, it shows how hard it is to be truly creative in developing novel ideas and converting them into innovative products.

Of course, not every organization has the resources to invest in basic R&D. As we've seen, a lot of this is done in universities, and is designed to explore fundamental issues about the nature of the world we live in and the way society works. Uncovering the secret of DNA wasn't done to enable the police to identify criminals, but the work that was done in identifying the double helix was essential for the eventual development of procedures for comparing the DNA found in tissue samples at a crime scene and comparing these to the DNA profiles of known criminals.

Activity 6

5 mins

What kind of fundamental research underpins the products or services your organization supplies? Think hard about it. You may not be able to pinpoint the specific research, but you may be able to identify what needed to be known for your organization to function as it does.

_____

_____

_____

_____

You may be surprised about some of the conclusions you reach. For example, most fast food and other catering outlets depend on frozen or chilled foods to be able to meet customer needs. How many people working in catering recognize that Francis Bacon (whose comments about innovation start this session) pioneered the technique? Bacon, an early 17th century natural philosopher, identified the preservative properties of the cold and died for his pains. (He contracted pneumonia when burying a chicken in snow to freeze it.)

In the same way, the binary system that is the basis of all modern computing is about three centuries old, and anthropologists have been investigating the belief systems, rituals and practices of other societies for well over 100 years and, in the process, can now help us to understand how people respond to advertising and marketing strategies in our own society.

The development of innovative products from fundamental research takes time, involves combining knowledge from different sources and disciplines and is often quite unpredictable. Looking back from the finished product it is clear how the basic ideas informed its development, but it wasn't obvious when those ideas were first being discussed.

However, there is far more effort these days to help convert fundamental research into products and services, or to improve their production and supply. This process is called _knowledge transfer_, and most universities and research institutes have systems and procedures to facilitate this process.

If knowledge transfer is the way that universities try to 'push' their research into marketable products and services, organizations' own R&D is the way that they try to pull those ideas from the other end. The best organizations, as we will see in Session C, encourage people to be alert to new ideas that could lead to them being able to offer new, better, more original products and services. This is what Bill Coyne, of 3M, calls empowerment, ensuring that people have the opportunity and the support to seek out new ideas and develop them successfully.

Case study

3M has set itself the goal of being at the leading edge of all the markets in which it operates, based on its substantial commitment to R&D. Two examples, about 50 years apart illustrate this.

In 1923, the US car industry had encouraged demand for two-tone cars (the top and bottom halves of the car body painted different colours). Existing car owners wanted garages to repaint half their car a different colour, done by masking off the half not being painted. The line between the two halves was marked sticky tape. When this was peeled off it took some paint with it, and this area had to be touched up to its original colour. Dick Drew, of 3M, was investigating how to improve the abrasives used to clean up the area before this was done. He recognized that if the paint wasn't removed in the first place the problem would be solved. After working for many months with experimental adhesives (for which there was no obvious use) he developed the product called masking tape that lacks the strong adhesive quality of other tapes, to meet the market need.

In the same way, and half a century later, Art Fry also worked at 3M and found a use for another weak adhesive to create what became Post-it™ notes. Both products relied on materials that had been rejected for their original purpose, to stick things together, because they didn't do so well enough. Yet it was the non-permanent features of both adhesives that made them ideal for their purpose.

Activity 7

What kind of R&D does your organization engage in? Does it have a formal R&D department or staff, does it buy in R&D from outside, or does it rely on new products or services emerging from managers and other employees?

_____

_____

If you work for a larger production organization then it will almost certainly have specialist R&D employees. Medium-sized production businesses often rely on outside resources with one or two internal specialists, who may have to combine R&D with other responsibilities. Smaller businesses, and many service-based organizations, lack a formal R&D process or personnel, although they may undertake or commission developmental activities that serve a similar purpose.

However, it's important that some form of R&D is undertaken if organizations are to survive in an increasingly competitive environment – and this applies as much in the public and voluntary sectors as it does in the private sector. It also needs to ensure that it encourages creativity and innovation in its R&D, and doesn't treat it as part of its continuous quality improvement process. Whilst continuous improvement is critical to long-term success, it's not sufficient on its own. Continuous improvement isn't necessarily innovative; innovation is not simply an improvement on what is currently being done but can be a complete and fundamental change in what the organization does.

Continuous improvement is mainly about ensuring that the organization meets current, identified customer requirements more effectively. Innovation often involves anticipating customer requirements, identifying products and services they haven't considered and meeting those. This means being prepared to take risks, and some industries and some organizations are far more risk averse than others. This means that they avoid taking risks.

This is particularly true for many public services, because they get no thanks for trying out risky ideas and getting them wrong. In the worst cases, innovation may cause harm to people. Taking risks with health care or education is likely to lead to condemnation if it goes wrong, so organizations tend to play safe.

Dominic Swords of the Innovation Research Centre at Henley Management Centre suggests that there is an important need for innovation, but it has to be in an appropriate context. He quotes an airline that publishes 'its commitment to getting it right first time, to continuous improvement and to innovation'. These three commitments can be thought of as sitting along a line from 'tight' to 'loose', reflecting the degree of organizational control needed to fulfil those values:

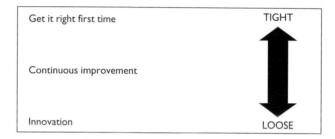

The significant question is:

'Which of these strategies would you want the pilot to use when landing the plane?'

Landing a plane full of people must be done right first time, every time. However, a test flight into the same airport might try an improved manoeuvre, and a test flight into an isolated and deserted airport may be the place for innovations in landing.

Getting it right first time means adhering to clear procedures and standards; continuous improvement can lead to improved procedures and higher standards over time, whilst innovation provides the breakthroughs which fundamentally re-shape procedures and set radically new standards. Each has its role, but at different times. Innovation isn't the only strategy for developing the organization, but an important one alongside the others.

Self-assessment 1

6 mins

1 Define:

Creativity: _____

Innovation: _____

2 What is the name for the problem organizations face in putting creative ideas into practice? _____

3 What are the six types of person identified by the diffusion of innovation curve?

(a) _____

(b) _____

(c) _____

(d) _____

(e) _____

(f) _____

Answers on page 73.

5 Summary

- Creativity is 'the thinking of novel and appropriate ideas' whereas innovation is 'the successful implementation of those ideas within an organization'.

- The problem many organizations face is the 'innovation gap', the gap between generating the creative idea in the first place and its implementation.

- The need for more innovation in organizations derives from greater wealth (so people are demanding more products and services) and greater expectations (as people demand better products and services), as more people are willing to try new things and they enter the mainstream more quickly (a steepening 'diffusion of innovation' curve).

- R&D become more important as organizations have to seek out new ideas and look for ways for converting them into marketable products and services.

- Innovation sits alongside continuous improvement in enabling organizations to meet customer needs, but involves far more fundamental changes than the incremental approach of continuous improvement.

Session B
Encouraging creativity

1 Introduction

'If at first, the idea is not absurd, there is no hope for it.'

Albert Einstein

In Session A, we saw that creativity is usually associated with artists and crafts-people but that everyone is capable of being creative, of thinking novel and appropriate ideas. Unfortunately most people lack the confidence to think such ideas, at least at work.

We spend so much of our lives learning to think and act conventionally, and to follow the rules and procedures the way that things have always been done. If you want to get people to think novel and appropriate ideas you need to create an environment in which this is seen to be possible. There are also a number of different techniques that you can use to encourage people to think of creative ideas, and in this session we will help you to use some of these techniques to encourage creativity in your team.

2 The innovation cycle

This session and Session C will use the idea of the *innovation cycle* to help you use creative techniques to finding innovative ways of resolving problems and developing news ways of working, new products and new services.

The innovation cycle involves four stages, and this session will focus on the first two of these:

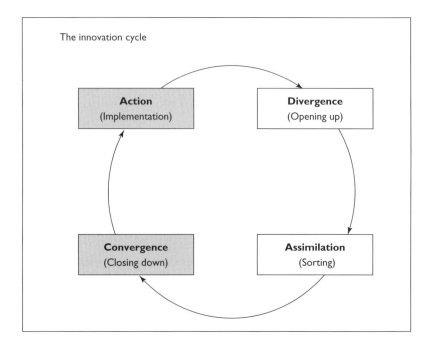

These four stages start with **Divergence**, the 'opening up' stage; this means encouraging people to come up with as many new and different ideas as they can, with no limit on imagination – the more outrageous the better. This is the chance to be creative, to look for ways of doing things which have never been thought of before because they turn received opinion upside down. Practicality must not be allowed to interfere with the generation of ideas, and quantity of ideas is better than quality.

Assimilation is the stage at which the ideas are sorted and their value is judged. It is important not to discard those which are different just because they are different but to sort through them and find the bits that are worth using. This is the stage which takes most time and is when the real breakthroughs can occur, when the impossible starts to be seen as the possible.

Some of the creative techniques (to encourage divergence) also have assimilation built in to them, others require it to be added on, as you will see.

It is valuable still to have more ideas than can actually be used after the assimilation stage for the move onto **Convergence** or 'closing down', deciding just what to go ahead with. The criteria for agreement before making the decision should be agreed, so the final choice is based on rational decisions and not just what people feel most comfortable with. The final stage is **Action**, implementing the decision.

The four creativity techniques we will look at in detail in this session are:

- Brainstorming
- TRIZ
- SCAMPER
- Synectics

We will also consider some variants on these, including Nominal Group Technique (NGT) and Trigger Sessions (variants on Brainstorming), and Lateral Thinking and Random juxtaposition (variants on Synectics).

3 Brainstorming

Brainstorming is probably the most widely used (and abused) technique for encouraging creative thinking. Is has been round for more than half a century, having been developed by American advertising man, Alex Osborn. He first described it in his 1948 book *Your Creative Power*.

Activity 8

3 mins

Have you ever taken part in a brainstorming session? What did you think about it? What rules (if any) were used to govern the activity?

_____

_____

_____

_____

Brainstorming is designed to be used with a group, ideally one that is large enough to include some diversity of experience and personality, but not so large that individuals may not get a chance to contribute. Around five to nine people are probably ideal. The rules (and there must be rules to make sure it works properly) are:

- Make sure that the purpose of the brainstorming session is clear and understood.
- Someone must control the group, to make sure that everyone takes part and nobody is allowed to dominate.

- Every idea is allowed, and is written down so that everyone can see it.
- Encourage people to build on the ideas of others (rather than discussing or objecting to them).

3.1 Make sure that the purpose of the brainstorming session is clear and understood

You may have heard that 'brainstorming' is offensive to people with certain conditions, particularly epilepsy. This isn't true and has explicitly been denied by the National Society for Epilepsy. A good manager always checks the facts before accepting rumour and hearsay.

The participants need to know what they are doing, and why. You may be trying to find creative solutions for a production or operational problem, such as repeated breakdowns of equipment or delays in meeting customer orders. You may be trying to develop new products or services for customers, or find ways of extending operational hours whilst giving greater flexibility of working conditions. This is the purpose of the brainstorming session, and it is useful to write this up on a whiteboard or flipchart in clear view of everybody the whole time they are developing creative ideas.

3.2 Someone must control the group, to make sure that everyone takes part and nobody is allowed to dominate

Start by explaining the rules of brainstorming so that everyone knows how they should behave. Watch who is contributing and encourage those who haven't said anything to do so. However, don't single people out. Some people have ideas but lack the confidence to call out. By asking them direct ('Any suggestions, Dianne?') they may feel safe to contribute. But don't challenge them to come up with something ('You've not said anything yet, Dianne. Come on, you must have some ideas.'). You won't encourage creativity by making people feel bullied.

On the other hand, don't allow someone to dominate. If one person keeps coming up with ideas, ask them to give others a chance to break in. If necessary, work round the group if everyone is itching to get their ideas heard.

3.3 Every idea is allowed, and is written down so that everyone can see it

Encourage people to call out their ideas, writing them down as they do so. This should be done so that everyone can read the ideas that have been generated. Again, a whiteboard or flipchart is useful for this.

3.4 Encourage people to build on the ideas of others (rather than discussing or objecting to them)

You should only allow anyone to query an idea if they haven't fully understood it. Otherwise, no discussion is allowed at this stage. If someone disagrees with an idea, then encourage them to suggest their own, contradictory idea.

If people seem to be running out of steam, set them a target – 'Ten more ideas before we stop.' You may be surprised at how people can generate ideas just to get the process completed, and come up with the most outrageous and creative ideas to do so.

There is one more feature of brainstorming that you should be aware of, and it's one that applies to most creative ideas generation. The physical environment needs to be right.

Activity 9 · 3 mins

What do you think are the ideal physical conditions for brainstorming to work well?

_____

_____

_____

_____

You may well have said that people should be sitting somewhere comfortable and, whilst the comfortable part is right, sitting isn't always the best way to generate creative ideas. You may find that by getting people to stand around the whiteboard or flipchart, even giving out pens to people, encourages them to be more creative.

They do need to have some privacy though. Other people mustn't be able to watch or hear what is going on, as that makes people self-conscious, which is the last thing you want if you are trying to encourage creativity. This is true for all the techniques we'll look at in this session. Creativity is about doing things differently, and repressing normal reservations about seeming to be a bit silly. This can't be done if other people can see and overhear what is being done.

The most important thing is for everyone to feel safe that they can let their brains loose without being made fun of! That requires mutual trust and confidence. That is something you need to be able to guarantee. Get everybody to agree that whatever anybody says or does, nobody will make fun of them. Instead they will try to outdo them in their creativity.

3.5 Variations on brainstorming

Brainstorming relies on the people taking part feeling confident to suggest ideas publicly. If the group contains both senior and junior staff, this may inhibit the freewheeling that is an important part of brainstorming. Ways to get round this include:

■ *Nominal Group Technique*

Developed by Andre Delbecq, Andrew Van de Ven and David Gustafson, NGT starts by people writing down their ideas (a sort of private brainstorm) and then sharing these with the group, in turn, so that each person reads out one idea. They go round again until everyone has completed their lists. Instead of the 'no discussion' rule of brainstorming, these ideas are discussed as they are described.

■ *Trigger Sessions*

Members of the group each write their ideas down on a sheet of paper and then pass this on to the next person. Having read someone else's ideas, people can add their own thoughts (triggered by these ideas) to the list, and pass this on again. The sheets get circulated until they are back where they started, or everyone runs out of ideas. This technique does allow duplication, so the different ideas are called out, in turn, round the table, people missing out any ideas from the list in front of them that have been said already.

A variant of this uses Post-it™ notes. Ideas are stuck up and read as people come up with them, and variants can be added. The advantage of this technique is that similar ideas can be physically grouped together to encourage development and refinement of the ideas.

4 TRIZ

TRIZ (pronounced TREEZ) is the acronym for the Russian name that translates as *Theory of Inventive Problem Solving*. It is a technique developed by the Russian engineer and patent expert Genrich Altshuller, who studied some 200,000 patents filed in the USSR. He concluded that the novel ideas that were the basis of these patents could be classified into 39 different categories. From this he identified 40 different strategies, called *inventive principles*, that could be used to encourage creative solutions to problems. These 40 principles are listed in the table below.

Although these principles apply mainly to manufacturing or engineering environments, some can be adapted to services as well. For example, a service could be modularized so that customers or users can combine elements to produce a customized version.

Activity 10

30 mins

Look through Altshuller's 40 Inventive Principles and see if you can think of any examples of this in your workplace:

Inventive principle	Our example	Your example
1. Segmentation – divide a product into sections that fit together	Modular units	
2. Extraction – remove something that is causing a problem	Straighten a bend where accidents occur	
3. Local quality – introduce variations to meet specific requirements of the environment	Colour coding in London underground trains to identify the line	
4. Asymmetry – make symmetrical objects asymmetric	Change the grip on a round handle to make it easier to hold firmly	
5. Combining – link together items that need to work together	TV with inbuilt DVD player	
6. Universality – multiple functions	Bed-settee	
7. Nesting – fit objects inside each other	Stackable furniture	
8. Counterweight – provide heavy objects with a lifting force	Hydraulic suspension	
9. Prior counter-action – anticipate a problem and build in the solution	Crumple-zones in cars to absorb force of collisions	
10. Prior action – design products so they are ready to use	Bread fingers and dips packaged together	

11. Cushion in advance – compensate for predictable problems	Heavy weights and large objects attached to hotel door keys to stop people leaving with them in their pockets	
12. Equi-potentiality – make it easier to access a product or component	Change the position of a component that will need to be replaced regularly	
13. Inversion – reverse a process to make it easier to do	A CD tray that slides out to enable the disk to be fitted securely	
14. Spheroidality – used curved rather than linear shapes or motions	Mouse ball converts linear into rotating motion	
15. Dynamicity – enable an object to change its shape or structure to meet different needs	The nose on Concorde rose up, reducing visibility, to enable supersonic flight after take off	
16. Partial or overdone action – where it is difficult to get the exact effect, do a little less or a little more than needed	Slightly overfill containers to ensure they are full, and capture and recycle the overflow	
17. Move to a new dimension – change the angle or plane of an object, or multi-layer it, to get desired effect	Printing one colour on top of another to get a full range of colours	
18. Mechanical vibration – shake an object	Vibrate moulds when filling them to ensure all internal areas are filled	
19. Periodic action – replace something continuous with something periodic	Flashing warning lights are more visible than constantly lit lights	
20. Continuous action – replace something periodic with something continuous	A saw blade cuts on forward and backward passes	
21. Rushing through – do something harmful or hazardous fast	Very fast cutter prevents the object deforming as it is cut	
22. Convert harm to benefit – make use of negative characteristics	Use of electric fences to control animals with low current shocks	

23. Feedback – control a process through feedback	Thermostats turn heat on and off in response to ambient temperature, rather than have continuous heating	
24. Mediator – use an intermediary to transfer something or carry out an action	Water pumped through central heating transfers heat from the boiler to rooms	
25. Self-service – use the object to service itself or add value to something else	Combined heat and power sources, using the heat from power generation to heat houses and offices	
26. Copying – use simple copies or images to replace complex, expensive or difficult objects	Models of police officers at road traffic blackspots encourage safer driving	
27. Cheap replacement use an inexpensive, short-lived object for expensive, durable one	Disposable nappies	
28. Replacement of a mechanical system by a system less likely to degrade through use	Laser disks (CDs and DVDs) replace vinyl records	
29. Pneumatic or hydraulic construction – replace mechanical parts with gas or liquid	Bubble wrap	
30. Flexible membranes or thin film – to protect or isolate an object from its environment	Cling film used to keep food fresh	
31. Use of porous material – to allow the object to interact with its environment or store liquids or gases	Racing cars use foam to store fuel as this is safer in an accident, reducing leakages	
32. Changing the colour of an object or its surroundings	Tool stores colour-coded fittings and tools to ensure items are stored in the right place	

33. Homogeneity – use the same or similar materials for different objects that interact	PTFE coated kitchen utensils don't scratch PTFE coated pans	
34. Rejecting and regenerating parts – remove or replace objects after use	Nylon line on strimmer that automatically feeds out more line	
35. Transform the physical/chemical states of an object	Pliable materials can be cooled to stiffen them to ease fitting	
36. Phase transformation – use the effect on an object as it absorbs heat or becomes louder	The movement of emergency vehicles causes their sirens to be heard better in front	
37. Thermal expansion – the expansion or contraction of materials as they heat or cool	Because different metals expand at different rates as they heat, by joining two such metals together they bend as they heat, to create switches	
38. Use strong oxidizers – use pure oxygen rather than ambient air to intensify an effect	Feeding oxygen to a welding torch to create greater heat	
39. Inert environment – change the normal environment to create one that is inert	Carbon dioxide fire extinguishers replace oxygen	
40. Composite materials – combine materials with different characteristics	Many composite materials that often combine lightness and flexible materials with strong, durable ones	

Clearly this is a long list, but it is long because it is comprehensive, so it provides a very useful checklist of techniques to solve problems creatively. The way that the TRIZ approach to creative problem solving works is to:

■ state the problem;

■ look for an analogous standard problem (i.e. a similar type of problem that has been solved elsewhere);

■ explore the solution to this analogous problem;

■ adapt this solution to your own problem.

The checklist helps you to identify the characteristics of the analogous solution so that you can apply this approach to your own problem. You will find that there are similarities between Altshuller's approach and the next two techniques we'll examine, SCAMPER and Synectics. SCAMPER uses a simpler list than TRIZ (six not 40 approaches) to identify potential solutions, and Synectics uses the idea of analogy to find a solution. You may find it easier to start with either of these at first, and build up to using TRIZ once you have got confident with either of them.

Altshuller went on to research the degree of inventiveness used in solving problems with products and processes, and found that there were five levels in the solutions being proposed. The table shows how common each of these five levels are:

Level	Level of inventiveness	Percentage of solutions	Source of knowledge
1	Routine solution, no novelty	32%	Personal knowledge
2	Minor improvement, some novelty	45%	Within organization
3	Major improvement, quite novel	18%	Within the industry
4	New concept, very novel	4%	Outside the industry
5	Discovery, radically new	1%	'All that is knowable'

In other words, about three-quarters of all problem solutions are reliant on little or no creativity and are unlikely to give the organization a significant advantage over others in the industry. Only 5% rely on ideas that are unknown in the industry, 1% of these being completely new ideas based on leading edge knowledge.

Activity 11

If you want to learn more about TRIZ, then you can follow up the topic by reading Extension 1.

Think about some recent problem-solving decisions in your organization. Which of these levels of inventiveness were apparent? Don't try and force them into a higher level than they are, but consider whether they reflect Altshuller's findings.

5 SCAMPER

SCAMPER stands for:

- **Substitute** components, materials, people or processes.

- **Combine** things or activities together.

- **Adapt** or change an activity or object.

- **Modify** something, making it bigger or smaller, change its shape or its features (e.g. its colour).

- **Put** something to another use.

- **Eliminate** something by removing components of stages in a process, simplify things and reduce them to their core functionality.

- **Reverse** something, turning inside out or upside down, or ask how you would do the reverse of what you want to do, to suggest how to do it better.

SCAMPER was developed by Bob Eberle, based on ideas originally put forward by Alex Osborn, the inventor of brainstorming. By using the checklist you can identify creative ways of addressing problems. What's more, the process applies in any kind of organization because it isn't manufacturing oriented.

Activity 12

7 mins

S/NVQ
C2

Think of a problem you face (or have faced) at work. Write the problem down and then use the SCAMPER approach to see what ideas you can come up with.

The problem:	
Substitute	
Combine	
Adapt	
Modify	
Put	
Eliminate	
Reverse	

6 Synectics

The term synectics to describe a creativity process stems from the book *Synectics: The Development of Creative Capacity* by W.J. Gordon, published in 1961. It is based on the principle of bringing together contradictory or very different ideas in order to generate a creative solution to a problem. It starts by detailed analysis and definition of the problem, on the grounds that you need to be very clear just exactly what it is or will finish up trying to solve the wrong problem or a symptom rather than a cause.

Solutions are generated based on analogies or metaphors – in other words, by looking for different situations where similar or equivalent problems exist and have been solved (like the analogous problems and solutions used in TRIZ). This can be helped by using triggers. These are words, phrases or ideas that may prompt people to think of analogies. What is important is that people feel able to identify analogies from quite different arenas. For example, triggers can include:

Subtract	Add	Transfer	Superimpose	Change	Scale
Substitute	Fragment	Isolate	Distort	Disguise	Contradict
Hybrid	Repeat	Combine	Parody	Mythology	Fantasize

Some of these triggers are similar to the list in SCAMPER, but others are more unusual, such as 'mythology' or 'fantasy'. Imagine you are trying to work out how to solve a security problem. In mythology this might be solved by invisibility or using giants as guards. From this analogy, the idea of disguising something so it isn't easy to see (invisibility) or using glass that magnifies guards may be considered.

The ideas are discussed in detail to refine them and make them manageable, but the key purpose of the synectics approach is that it encourages a very creative approach to problem solving by combining the unreal or impractical with the real problem to come up with a viable solution.

Activity 13

S/NVQ C2

Look at the problem you considered in Activity 12. Think of a mythological or fantastic analogy, where the same or a similar problem occurred. Use this to try and generate a viable solution:

The problem:
Mythological or fantastic analogy:
Possible solution based on this:

Similar ideas to synectics include:

■ *Lateral thinking*

Developed by Edward de Bono, lateral thinking encourages people to look for solutions to problems that don't fit into the fixed mindsets that often condition our thinking. Mindsets are the way that we have always done things or approached issues, and these limit our ability to see things from new perspectives. De Bono has written several books on this approach.

■ *Random juxtaposition*

This is a fancy name for a simple technique that uses random words or ideas to encourage people to look for links between the idea and the problem. The random words can come from a dictionary (or any book in fact). Just open it at any page and use the first word on that page. Like synectics, the challenge is to find a link between the random word and the issue being considered.

7 Assimilation

All these different techniques — brainstorming, TRIZ, SCAMPER, synectics, and their variants — have one thing in common. They try to encourage people to think 'outside the box'. Outside the box simply means not thinking in conventional ways or doing things the same way as always. Creativity is about novelty, about doing things that haven't been done before.

If you start from the point of view that everyone is able to be creative, if they have the opportunity and the encouragement, then you are more likely to generate creative ideas. So, the first step in using any of these creative ideas generation techniques is to believe that they are going to work.

The second step is to use them carefully. Far too many people ignore the rules of brainstorming:

■ Make sure that the purpose of the brainstorming session is clear and understood.

■ Someone must control the group, to make sure that everyone takes part and nobody is allowed to dominate.

■ Every idea is allowed, and is written down so that everyone can see it.

■ Encourage people to build on the ideas of others (rather than discussing or objecting to them).

Remember Altshuller's findings, that most new ideas are really only the reworking of existing ideas, and that most don't give an organization any real advantage over their competitors. This reflects failure of most organizations to treat creativity (and innovation) seriously. They assume that saying they want creative ideas is the same as working hard to generate them.

So the third step is treat creative ideas generation as a critical task. Prepare properly and develop your knowledge and skills in using these techniques. Some are more demanding than others, so start with what you feel comfortable doing. A technique like SCAMPER is often easiest if you are looking at a quality problem and want a creative solution. It is a clear and fairly simple technique to use. Although brainstorming looks easy, it is often done badly because it does require that you keep the process under control and to the rules. It can be difficult to keep up with the ideas if people get enthused.

Although it looks complicated, TRIZ is a very structured technique that you will find that your team will soon understand. It is designed to work with manufacturing or production activities, but does also work in services. Synectics is probably the most demanding in that you rely heavily on the participants to get actively involved, but if they have done some brainstorming they will rise to the challenge of trying to link up quite different ideas or objects in creative ways.

Both TRIZ and Synectics have assimilation built into their processes, TRIZ in the fourth stage (adapt this solution to your own problem) and Synectics through the discussion that takes place after the extreme analogies have been generated (this is also true for NGT, where discussion is built into the process).

Brainstorming specifically discourages discussion, so you will need to move on to examine the ideas that have been generated as a separate stage. This is also true of Lateral Thinking and Random juxtaposition. One way of organizing the assimilation process is to transfer the list of ideas to Post-it™ notes and get the group to physically sort these, to find linkages. They can also show how valid they think ideas are by placing them centrally in a group or on the periphery.

SCAMPER is really a structured form of Brainstorming and the rules of Brainstorming also apply, but the SCAMPER process tends to build in assimilation, through the structure it uses.

Activity 14

S/NVQ
C2

Think about the four techniques we have looked at, and the other variants as well, and decide which one you are going to try out. Plan your session carefully, make sure the environment is appropriate and that you have the resources you need.

Try out the technique and write down your thoughts on how it went here.

What was the problem?

_____

_____

What technique did you use?

_____

What went well when you used it?

_____

_____

_____

_____

What areas do you need to improve on?

_____

_____

_____

_____

Did you come up with some useful ideas as a result?

_____

Looking at Altshuller's five levels of creativity, where would you place the best idea(s)?

Level	Level of inventiveness	Source of knowledge	Your solutions
1	Routine solution, no novelty	Personal knowledge	
2	Minor improvement, some novelty	Within organization	
3	Major improvement, quite novel	Within the industry	
4	New concept, very novel	Outside the industry	
5	Discovery, radically new	'All that is knowable'	

If you want to learn more about the techniques we have looked at in this session, you will find Tony Proctor's book (Extension 2) very useful.

In Session C, we will look at how you convert creative ideas into successful solutions and what makes some organizations good at it, and some less good.

Self-assessment 2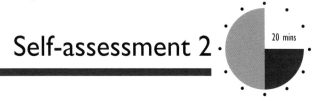

1   Complete the empty boxes in this diagram of the innovation cycle

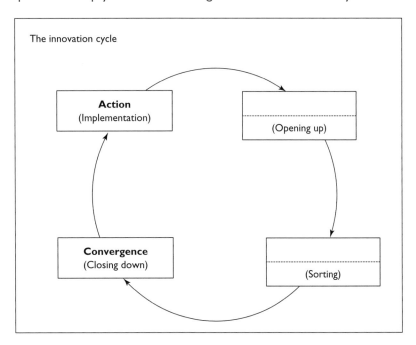

2   What are the four rules of brainstorming?

   1

   2

   3

   4

3   What are the two variants on brainstorming called?

   1

   2

4   What does the acronym TRIZ stand for (in English)?

_____

5   What do the five Inventive principles mean in practice?

   1 Segmentation

_____

   2 Extraction

_____

   3 Local quality

_____

   4 Asymmetry

_____

   5 Combining

_____

6   What are the four stages in the TRIZ problem-solving process?

   1

   2

   3

   4

7   What percentage of solutions to problems did Altshuller find were radically new discoveries?

_____

8 What does SCAMPER stand for?

S

C

A

M

P

E

R

9 What is the principle underpinning Synectics?

_____

_____

10 List two other techniques similar to Synectics:

1

2

Answers on pages 74–5.

8 Summary

- Brainstorming is probably the most widely used (and abused) technique for encouraging creative thinking. It is based on four rules:

  - Make sure the purpose is clear and understood
  - Control the group, make sure everyone takes part and nobody dominates
  - Every idea is allowed and written up for all to see
  - Build on the ideas of others, don't discuss or object to them.

- Two other techniques that are similar to brainstorming for encouraging creative ideas are NGT and Trigger Sessions.

- TRIZ (Theory of Inventive Problem Solving) was based on research into patents, and has identified 40 basic approaches to creative problem solving.

- TRIZ involves a four-stage process for problem solving:

  - State the problem
  - Look for an analogous standard problem
  - Explore the solution to this analogous problem
  - Adapt this solution to your own problem.

- Altshuller found that there was little real inventiveness in most solutions to problems, with 32% offering only a routine solution with no novelty, and 45% only minor improvements showing some novelty. Eighteen per cent were quite novel major improvements, only 4% involved a really novel concept, and just 1% involved a radically new discovery.

- SCAMPER is a checklist of ideas for generating creative solutions to problems. It stands for Substitute, Combine, Adapt, Modify, Put, Eliminate or Reverse.

- Synectics is based on bringing together contradictory or very different ideas in order to generate a creative solution to a problem.

- Two techniques similar to synectics are Lateral thinking (developed by Edward de Bono) and Random juxtaposition.

- The three steps to using any creative ideas generation technique is:

  - Believe that they are going to work.
  - Use them carefully, keeping to the rules.
  - Treat creative ideas generation as a critical task.

Session C
Encouraging innovation

1 Introduction

In this session we will look at how you can turn creative ideas into innovative processes, products and services. Before we do so, here are some examples of the kind of thinking that stifles innovation and creativity:

- 'This "telephone" has too many shortcomings to be seriously considered as a means of communication. The device is inherently of no value to us.' Western Union internal memo, 1876
- 'Who … wants to hear actors talk?' H. M. Warner, Warner Brothers, 1927
- 'We don't like their sound, and guitar music is on the way out.' Decca Recording Company executive rejecting the Beatles, 1962
- 'There is no reason anyone would want a computer in their home.' Ken Olson, president, chairman and founder of Digital Equipment Corporation, 1977

No matter how effective you and the people you lead are at developing creative ideas, the chance of you being able to implement them depends on your organization being receptive to them. In this final session we will look at the last two stages of the innovation cycle, Convergence and Action. It is at these two stages that you have to identify what will work in your organization, and how you can make it work. We will look at some of the techniques you can use for judging what is likely to work and how; we will also look at how you can judge whether or not your organization is capable of accepting innovative ideas.

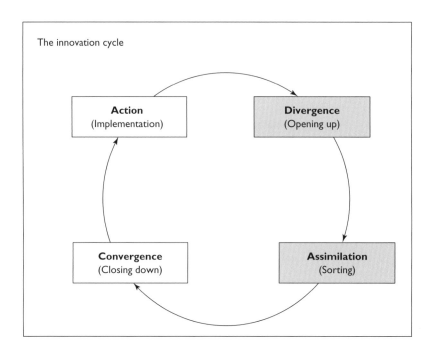

The innovation cycle

Action (Implementation)
Divergence (Opening up)
Convergence (Closing down)
Assimilation (Sorting)

2 Convergence

Convergence is the closing down process, when all the ideas that have been developed and sorted during the first two stages are judged and decisions made about their viability. Viability means deciding two things:

1   Would they work?

2   Can this organization make them work?

If you think these are the same thing, look at the quotations that start this session. Western Union was a telegraph company, and failed to recognize the potential of the telephone. It is now primarily a money transfer business, and discontinued telegrams this year. Although one of the Warner Bros. did not see the potential of talkies, others did, and Warner Bros. produced the first feature film with a soundtrack, in 1927, called The Jazz Singer.

Decca had been the UK's largest record label, and although the company rejected The Beatles it did sign The Rolling Stones (on George Harrison's recommendation). They left subsequently and the label went into decline during the 1970s, as did its classical arm. However, it has managed to revive this side of its business. Nevertheless, the rejection of The Beatles was symptomatic of an organization that was not in tune with changes in its main market.

The Digital Equipment Corporation (DEC) was very successful in producing mini-computers for scientists and engineers during the 1970s and 1980s but failed to recognize the impact of the PC and eventually had to be sold to Compaq, a company that was in itself taken over by Hewlett Packard.

It's easy, in retrospect, to point the finger at people who failed to see innovative opportunities when they were first offered to them. Many smart people have made the same mistake. After all, when Fred Smith wrote a paper proposing a reliable overnight delivery service, his Yale University management professor said: 'The concept is interesting and well-formed, but in order to earn better than a "C," the idea must be feasible.' Smith went on to found Federal Express!

Activity 15

3 mins

Has your organization ever rejected an innovation or have you or your colleagues ever looked at what another organization in the industry has done and said: 'It'll never work!' Were you right?

_____

_____

Making a judgement about a creative idea is hard, and the more creative the idea, the more different it is from what is considered normal, the more likely you are to reject it. You wouldn't be alone. An American philosopher of science, Thomas Kuhn, described the difficulty that many scientists had accepting new ideas, and these are people who are supposedly constantly seeking new ideas. He described what he called 'paradigms'. These are accepted ways of thinking and doing things, the explanation that is broadly accepted as the right one in any scientific community.

Most science is based on theories that are hard to prove, but which become accepted as the best explanation available, until someone comes up with an alternative. Unfortunately, many people have made their names and their careers based on the old theories, so they have a vested interest in rejecting the new ideas.

What tends to happen is that only a few scientists support the new idea (like the Innovators and Early Adopters we met in Session A). However, it can take some time to win over the rest of the community, and some 'Laggards' will never accept them. This has been true for centuries, and Kuhn argued that it takes time for the old paradigm to be replaced with a new one that will probably be just as resistant to change as the one it replaced.

Activity 16

You may well have seen major changes in your organization or another during your working life. Did you see some people who welcomed the change but others who resisted it, some right up until the end? What was your experience like?

_____

_____

_____

_____

Kuhn's idea of paradigms and what he calls paradigm shifts (the change to a new paradigm) is just as common in other areas of our lives. Getting people to accept creative ideas and the innovation that flows from it is often difficult. People who believe that what they are doing is right and worthwhile will find it difficult to accept changes.

How do you make sure that you don't reject creative ideas simply because they don't fit into your personal paradigm? The way to do it is establish rules to answer the question about your ideas:

■ 'Would they work?'

Later in this session, when we get onto looking at how you implement the ideas we'll consider the other question:

■ 'Can this organization make them work?'

3 *Closing down* techniques

There are several techniques you can use to help you judge the ideas that have come out of a creative ideas process. The main ones are:

■ Hurdles
■ Ranking
■ Weighting
■ Instinct

Before we look at these in detail, let's just look at why you need to go through this process. Creative ideas generation is all about coming up with ideas that are different, novel ideas that haven't been thought of before. They don't need to be easily implemented – in fact, in the early stages, the best ones just won't work at all. Creativity is all about breaking free from conventional thinking and not allowing yourselves to be constrained by what has been done or even what could be done.

The assimilation stage, when you sort ideas is the point at which discussion can help you to find practical ways of making them work, closing the gap between what would be nice to do, and what is doable. However, you should not allow yourselves to discuss which idea is better, only whether you can use the ideas. By holding off deciding which idea to take up until now you allow the more extreme ideas to sink in and become less threatening for people.

Now, by closing down on the most suitable ideas, you can focus on what will best meet your needs. This means looking at the ideas from the point of view of the problem to be solved, of the customer need to be met, and so on. These closing down techniques help you focus on that in making your decisions.

3.1 Hurdles

Imagine a hurdle race on a course where all the hurdles are different heights. The first hurdle is quite low, but the hurdles get progressively higher, until only the very best hurdlers can manage them. Hurdles in decision making work the same way, by setting increasingly difficult constraints which the creative ideas must meet to be selected.

Activity 17 · 5 mins

An insurance company wants to persuade its customers to buy extra products from its telephone sales service. It is looking at a range of financial products that it could offer, after a brainstorming session that has come up with a list of possible services.

It has decided to set some hurdles that the products must jump over if they are to be selected. These are listed below, in no specific order. Sort them into what you believe would be an appropriate order, from the most basic that the new services must meet, to those which might be the basis for making the final decision between whatever is left.

Hurdles	**Your order for the hurdles, from most basic at the top to the final discriminator at the bottom**
Financial Services Authority must be prepared to licence us to offer it	
We must already have the skills to offer it	
Customers must think us a suitable source	
Must be able to be supplied via the Internet	
No other organizations dominate the market	

Compare your order to ours, on page 77.

Hurdles reflect what is important to you as an organization. By starting with those that are absolutely basic, you ensure that you have relevant ideas. The subsequent hurdles help you to identify those ideas that will really add some value to your processes, products or services. By focusing on what you need from the creative ideas, rather than how well they match what you have done before, you allow yourself to assess each idea on its merits, not how conventional it is.

3.2 Ranking

Ranking is similar to using hurdles, but is done by comparison of the ideas. It is particularly useful if there is one significant criterion that you have to try and meet, but one which is hard to quantify or measure. That means you are having to rely on judgements.

Criterion is the singular of *criteria*. With two or more ways of deciding you have criteria, but with just one it is a criterion.

You need to start by determining what the criterion is that you want to use in choosing your rank order, such as:

■ Removes as much of the problem as possible.
■ Is completely different from our main competitors.
■ Would add real value in the eyes of our customers.

Then, take any two of the ideas and decide which best meets that criterion and place it above the other on a whiteboard or wall (Post-it™ notes are really useful for this task). Select any one of the remaining ideas and decide where it fits – above, below or between the first two. Carry on placing all the ideas on the list until you have them listed in rank order.

(Note: This technique doesn't require you to decide how much better one idea is than another, just that it is.)

Activity 18

A mail order company gets complaints from customers about orders being delivered when nobody is at home. They get a card and have to call the delivery company and arrange another delivery when someone will be at home, or at an alternative address or collect the goods themselves from a depot. As well as irritating customers, this adds to the price charged by the delivery company. Unfortunately the items are expensive and have to be signed for to prove delivery.

The ideas that have been suggested to overcome this are listed below. They need to be ranked in order, from the top to the bottom, based on this criterion, that it maximizes the number of successful first time deliveries.

The ideas	**Your rank order**
Use a tamper-proof container that can be locked to the letterbox with a release code that can be sent by text when the person requests it	
Deliver in the evenings and weekends	
Offer to deliver to workplaces	
Use local delivery points, such as post offices, for people to collect their items in their own time	
Ask for a neighbour's name and address as an alternative delivery address	

Compare your order to ours, on page 77.

3.3 Weighting

Weighting is a bit like hurdles, but instead of eliminating the ideas in turn, you give points to each one on the basis of what characteristics it possesses (or take them away if it's an undesired characteristic). The more weights that an idea has, the better.

The advantage of this technique is that it allows you to show the relative importance of the different characteristics you are looking for by using different weights. You can give one point for each, or one for some, two, three or more for others.

Activity 19 · 5 mins

The insurance company in Activity 17 has decided to use weights instead to close down on the different ideas. Look at each criterion and decide whether you would weight some more than others.

Characteristics	Your weights for each
Financial Services Authority must be prepared to licence us to offer it	
We must already have the skills to offer it	
Customers must think us a suitable source	
Must be able to be supplied via the Internet	
No other organizations dominate the market	

Compare your weights to ours, on page 78.

3.4 Instinct

Sometimes, no matter how hard you try, you can't determine which is the best idea. In that case, when all else fails, use your instincts. Ask yourself 'What feels right?' However, you must remember what Thomas Kuhn taught us, that we often find it hard to accept something that completely upsets our views on what is right.

Look at each idea and try to see them as if you had no experience of the organization, the industry or the market. Which idea really looks as if it will do what you want it to? Above all, which idea is most likely to work in the future when other things may have changed as well?

4 Action: organizational readiness for innovation

How easy is it for your organization to make innovative ideas happen? As we learnt in Session A, a report from the Centre for Exploitation of Science and Technology (CEST) distinguished two types of technical innovation, between:

- *evolutionary innovation*, taking the design of existing practices, products or services a step further away from conventional ways of doing things, which is undertaken on a planned basis, or

- *revolutionary innovation*, based on 'serendipity' (an opportunity for innovative practices, products or services occurring) which cannot be predicted but which the organization must be alert to and supportive of when the occasion arises.

We said then that an organization that wasn't prepared to accept evolutionary innovations was unlikely to be ready to accept revolutionary ideas. How ready is your organization for either? A study of 250 European organizations in the early 1990s suggested that there are three core competences required for innovation:

1 *Technological*: the ability to develop new ways of working and new products or services.

2 *Entrepreneurial*: the willingness to try out new ideas and take risks.

3 *Learning*: the ability to learn from the experience of developing innovative ways of working, and new products or services (and, in the latter case, taking them to market).

Learning ability is all about being able to achieve success in the marketplace. It is all very well being able to develop new ways of working and new products or services but these must also find favour with the organization's customers. The University of Sussex Science Policy Research Unit in its 'Project Sappho' identified five factors associated with organizations achieving commercial success with technical innovation, factors that indicate their learning ability:

- They understand user needs.

- They pay attention to marketing.

- Development work is undertaken efficiently (but not necessarily more quickly).

- They make effective use of external technical advice.

- Responsibility for innovation is at a senior level with more authority.

A similar set of findings came from a study of Microsoft's approach to innovation in designing new software. The research, by Michael Cusumano of the Sloan School of Management at the Massachusetts Institute of Technology (MIT), identified five key features in their strategy:

- Hire the best people from Universities and from other companies. (Best doesn't just mean technically highly qualified but those who demonstrate that they can apply their knowledge in practical, market-led ways.)

- Avoid compartmentalization. (Mix together project teams, including Marketing, so that development is led by what the market requires, and that Marketing staff only sell what is actually deliverable.)

- Don't be ambitious. (Only design simple features into new products and then develop them continuously to make them more complex later. This avoids risk, cuts down development time – the time it takes to get from a creative idea to the market – and simplifies the development process.)

- Parallel development. (Multiple teams work on different aspects of the software, meeting frequently to synchronize development, rather than developing sequentially across a broad front, progressing through a series of separate stages.)

- Enable developers to learn from their successes and failures. (Use mechanisms like *post-mortems* to find out where things went right and wrong.)

Finally, we'll look at the 3M Corporation. Bill Coyne, who we first met in Session A, identified six characteristics of 3M which, he suggests have enabled the company to be regarded as innovatory, despite their size and age as a corporation. These characteristics are:

1 Vision	Not just a sense of purpose but a purpose which explicitly includes innovation and one which is constantly translated into practice by employees. Vision is 'where we want to go'!
2 Foresight	The ability to predict accurately where customers are going, how they will react to the changing environment in which they live. It involves identifying their needs, both the *articulated need*, reflecting problems which customers are aware of (e.g. to replace CFC as a propellant in aerosols), and *unarticulated needs*, those requiring a real insight into the customers' situation (e.g. the need seen by Dick Drew in 1923 for masking tape in vehicle repainting or Art Fry's application of a low adhesive to notelets which produced Post-it™ notes). The difficulty of identifying these unarticulated needs can be reduced by seeking out lead users – those people whose exacting demands

and advanced applications of products tell you something about the likely direction the industry is taking.

3 Stretch goals

Vision and foresight help to set a culture of innovation, but people need to be pushed to go beyond simple incremental improvements. 3M's stretch goals include:

- 30% of sales to be from products introduced in last 4 years;
- 10% of sales to be from products introduced in last year.

This creates a sense of urgency; innovation is time sensitive, missing market opportunity can seriously reduce profitability.

4 Empowerment

This means more than empty rhetoric – it means giving people some say over how they use their time. At 3M technical staff have the right to spend up to 15% of their time on projects of their own choosing. This is not measured but is a notional concept which creates a climate in which individual initiative is positively expected – a form of institutionalized revolution! For every 1,000 ideas, only 100 become formal proposals, and only a few of these new product ventures – of which over half fail.

5 Communication

This means creating an open organization in which horizontal contact and networking is possible, enabling multi-disciplinary teams to be created and the cross-fertilization of ideas to occur. Many new ideas involve the application of exiting technologies to new product areas. This communication is based on three ground rules:

(a) products belong to divisions but technologies belong to the company;

(b) multiple methods for sharing information, including technical fairs and forums managed by the technical staff, plus technical audits to identify technology transfer possibilities;

(c) staff are told that networking is their responsibility, but communication systems and the 15% rule facilitate that process.

| 6 Rewards and recognition | Award programmes covering innovation, often based on peer recognition, and promotion on a dual ladder to either advanced technical grades or to management posts (but not direct financial rewards for specific innovations – that's their job!). |

There are similarities between all these lists of characteristics. They suggest that any organization that is ready to embrace innovation must probably have the following characteristics:

- The technical ability to develop new ways of working and new products or services, including a commitment to recruit knowledgeable, skilled people and continue to invest in their training.
- The entrepreneurial will to try out new ideas and take risks, with a commitment from the top of the organization to encourage creativity and innovation.
- The ability to learn from experience, both successes and failures, with systems to review what happened and a culture that encourages honesty in doing it.
- An understanding of the (current and potential future) needs of users (customers, clients, patients, etc.) and an emphasis on finding out what users require and striving to meet this.
- Pay attention to marketing, with people from marketing or the customer facing part of the organization involved in development alongside all the people affected by the development.
- Development work is undertaken efficiently (but not necessarily more quickly) through collaborative working, drawing on external technical advice where necessary.
- A strong commitment to evolutionary development ('Don't be ambitious') but a willingness to seize opportunities when they arise (and the wisdom to see when it wouldn't be sensible to do so).

Activity 20

Carry out an assessment of your organization. How ready is it to embrace innovation and make it happen? You may need to talk to some of your colleagues about this, to get a complete picture.

There are five possible choices for each characteristic. The following explains each in a little more detail:

- Excellent: we really do set the standard by which other organizations judge themselves.

- Very good: we're up with the leaders but not the best.

- OK, but we need to improve: we try, but do need to get better at this if we are to survive in the long term.

- Not very good at all: we really do need to get our act together.

- Hopeless: we have no appreciation of the importance of this.

Characteristics	Excellent	Very good	OK, but we need to improve	Not very good at all	Hopeless
Technical ability to innovate, based on recruiting and training the best people					
Entrepreneurial will and commitment from the top to encourage creativity and innovation					
The ability to learn from experience					
Understanding of and commitment to meet the current and future needs of users					
Attention to marketing in the development of innovative processes, products and services					
Efficient development using through collaborative working and external technical advice, where necessary					
Commitment to evolutionary development and a willingness to select appropriate opportunities when the arise					

5 Action: planning implementation

All changes need to be properly planned, and innovative change is no exception. There is more about planning change in the Super Series workbook *Planning Change*, but there are a few specific issues that are particularly important if the change is going to be innovative. According to US academic Rosabeth Moss Kanter in her influential book *The Change Masters* (Allen & Unwin, 1983), the power to bring about innovatory change relies on:

- Information (data, technical knowledge and expertise, political intelligence)
- Resources (funds, materials, space, staff, time)
- Support (endorsement, backing, approval, legitimacy)

The first of these, information, means that managers must ensure that they possess knowledge about the nature of the new processes, products or services that they are proposing to introduce. They should as individuals or, preferably, as a group, set out to be the authorities on the issue involved and on its implementation. They need to take full advantage of being a group by seeking knowledge and sharing it, taking responsibility for investigating particular areas and becoming the 'group expert' on that, identifying sources, making contacts and undertaking reading. The sum of all the individual expertise generated will be greater than the amount each individual could hope to develop in the time and with the resources available.

Secondly, you need resources, and whatever resources are needed, there will never be enough! Managers must identify what resources there are available and make the fullest use of them and build alliances to share resources from other sources. They shouldn't attempt to duplicate what is being done elsewhere in the organization, but look for ways of opening things up to get more out of whatever is happening there. The time available must be used as effectively as possible by planning activities, allocating targets and reviewing progress on a regular basis, not getting side-tracked and allowing interesting activities to distract them from important ones.

Finally, according to Kanter, you will need support. If you want to bring about innovation in your organization you must either possess the power to do so yourself (and most first line managers only have limited power to innovate), or you must identify who has the power to make things happen (and who has the power to prevent it) and get them to act as your sponsor. This means finding out what their priorities are and working to them. If you challenge someone else's aims or values, you won't build alliances. If you are part of a team trying to introduce an innovative new way of working, or innovative products or services, team's power is likely to be *derived* power. This means that it is derived from the senior manager(s) who have sponsored and supported the project.

Activity 21

10 mins

S/NVQ C2

Think about these three requirements for successfully implementing innovation (information, resources and support). Review your organization and your own skills in gaining all three and identify what you might need to do to improve your access to them:

1 *Information*

■ What systems and procedures exist in my organization for accessing information? How effective are they? How can I access them?

_____

_____

_____

_____

■ How good am I at accessing information in order to become knowledgeable about a topic? What skills and knowledge do I need to develop to improve my ability?

_____

_____

_____

_____

2 *Resources*

■ How are resources for the development of innovative processes, products and services controlled and allocated? What would I have to do to get access to them? Who would I need to build alliances with if I were to want access to resources for any particular innovative developments?

_____

_____

_____

_____

■ How good am I at controlling the use of resources, including my own time? How good am I at building alliances? What skills and knowledge do I need to develop to improve my ability?

_____

_____

_____

_____

3   *Support*

■ Where does power lie in my organization, whose support would I need for different areas in which I might want to develop innovative processes, products and services?

_____

_____

_____

_____

■ How much power do I have? What kinds of innovative developments to processes, products and services can I introduce without being too dependent on others? How good am I at getting the support of others? What skills and knowledge do I need to develop to improve my ability?

_____

_____

_____

_____

6 Action: implementing innovation

If you want to bring about real innovation, and you have obtained the information, resources and support that you need, you then need to think 'How am I actually going to do it?' There are three possible ways you can go about putting your innovation into practice:

■ Mission–oriented

■ Negotiation

■ Action research

6.1 Mission-oriented

A Mission-oriented strategy means that it is possible to link the innovation explicitly to the mission of the organization (or department), or to a specific current objective. The advantage of such an approach is that there is less need to present arguments for why the innovation should be allowed, merely to argue why this is better than any alternatives.

Of course, this assumes that the mission is both clear about what the organization is all about and is respected. Neither is always the case!

Activity 22 · 3 mins

What is your organization's mission?

_____

_____

Do people readily know this? Is it influential in how the organization works and what it does?

_____

_____

Even if the mission isn't always that relevant or important, you may find specific business objectives that the innovation supports, and they can provide the basis for your implementation.

6.2 Negotiation

A Negotiation strategy is useful when the innovation doesn't clearly derive from a mission statement (or the mission statement is not given much weight) and it cuts across different departments or areas of the organization, and so doesn't fit neatly into one manager's business objectives.

You will need to build consensus around the innovation and persuade different people that it fits into their goals in different ways. You may well have to resolve conflicts between these different areas or goals, as people compete to fit your innovation into their particular needs, sometimes reducing its innovative qualities in the process.

Activity 23

3 mins

Have you had experience of any developments in your organization that have cut across internal boundaries? How easily did this occur? Is there a tendency for internal competition or are people willing to work collaboratively on activities that may affect them differently?

6.3 Action research

Action research is a far less common approach to introducing innovation. It places the emphasis of implementation on the *process* rather than the *outcome*. It is useful when an innovation involves doing things that are so different that you are not altogether clear how they will work. The creative idea may be sound but you need to work out how to do it *as* you do it. This may sound a bit scary, to start off doing something when you aren't clear how it will turn out, but Action research is all about learning.

Organizations that are willing to accept this approach tend to be those which are either very open to innovation and prepared to take risks in order to be at the leading edge, and those which are struggling to find a solution to a problem that is so large that they will accept Action research because there is no alternative open to them.

Activity 24

3 mins

How do you think your organization would react to the idea of Action research? Which of the two conditions (a risk taking organization or one that is struggling with problems) is a better description of it?

How would you feel about setting out to introduce something when you weren't very clear what it was you were introducing?

_____

_____

6.4 Expect resistance to innovation

All change is threatening for people and innovative change is even more threatening. Resistance to innovation reflects the dominant mind-sets in the organization (the way people think the conventional wisdom about what is possible). These create self-imposed barriers to change, often based on assumptions about how effective existing approaches are and new approaches will be.

This kind of thinking is characterized by 'one-correct answer' thinking – the attitude of mind that assumes that there is only one way to do things, and that's the way we have always done it. People are reluctant to challenge the way they have always done things ('it ain't broke so don't fix it') and are immediately negative about anything new ('we tried that once and it didn't work').

Worst still, if the ideas have been developed outside the organization, by consultants, technical experts or through imitating what a leading edge competitor is doing, you may meet the 'not invented here' syndrome. Since it comes from outside it won't work here 'because we're different'.

All this does is to emphasize how much people fear looking foolish by trying something new and failing. As Tom Peters says (in _Thriving On Chaos_), the worst kind of organization is the one that doesn't make mistakes, as mistakes come from taking risks, and long-term success is dependent on risk-taking. All mistakes are a chance to learn, and the successful organization celebrates failure the first time it happens, so that it can learn and repeat the mistake.

Activity 25 · 3 mins

How do you think you can overcome this kind of resistance?

_____

_____

_____

_____

There are several strategies you can follow to overcome this kind of resistance. The first is to make sure that you involve people right from the start, so that they take part in developing the innovation. It is useful to identify the people who are most likely to be resistant and bring them on board as early as possible.

Secondly, choose the implementation strategy – Mission-oriented, Negotiation or Action research – to fit the situation. If your innovation clearly moves the organization forwards in its mission, then make that the centrepiece of your approach. If it involves different parts of the organization, make sure you understand their goals and work with them not against them. If you need to use an Action research approach, then make sure the likeliest pockets of resistance are fully involved in the process.

Thirdly, remember Rosabeth Moss Kanter's advice – make yourself and your implementation team the organization's experts on the subject, so people can't blind you with their knowledge. Make sure you have the resources you need to make it happen. Try not to get into the situation where you are dependent on other people for permission to use the resources you need, because that gives them the power of veto over what you do. Finally, get the support of key people, so that you get the power to make things happen despite resistance, if necessary.

Self-assessment 3

20 mins

1 Complete the empty boxes in this diagram of the innovation cycle.

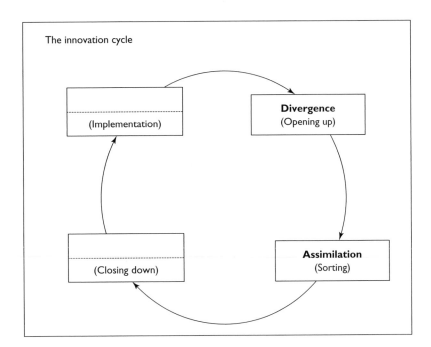

The innovation cycle

(Implementation)

Divergence
(Opening up)

(Closing down)

Assimilation
(Sorting)

2 What are the two questions you should ask to decide on the viability of creative ideas?

1

2

3 What did Thomas Kuhn call the dominant mind-set that shapes how scientists respond to new ideas?

4 Name four techniques you could use to judge the ideas from the creative ideas process?

5 What are the two types of technical innovation identified by CEST?

6 What are the three core competences required for innovation?

7 Complete the following:

Any organization that is ready to embrace _____ must have the _____ ability to develop new ways of working and new products or services, the _____ will to try out new ideas and take risks, the ability to _____ from experience, and an understanding of the needs of _____. They also pay attention to _____, their development work is undertaken _____ and they have a strong commitment to _____ development.

8 According to Rosabeth Moss Kanter, the power to bring about innovatory change relies on what three factors?

1

2

3

9 What are the three main approaches to implementing innovations in organizations?

The answers to these questions can be found on pages 75–6.

7 Summary

- The four stages of the innovation cycle are divergence, assimilation, convergence and action.

- In assessing the likelihood of any creative ideas being viable, a manager should ask:

  - Would they work?
  - Can this organization make them work?

- The US philosopher of science Thomas Kuhn described the dominant mind-set that shapes how scientists respond to new ideas as a paradigm, a concept that helps to explain why people react to creativity and innovation the way they do.

- There are four techniques that can be used in deciding which creative ideas to use:

  - Hurdles
  - Ranking
  - Weighting
  - Instinct

- The two types of technical innovation identified by Centre for Exploitation of Science and Technology are *evolutionary innovation* and *revolutionary innovation*.

- The three core competences required by organizations wishing to introduce innovation are *technological ability*, *entrepreneurial ability* and *learning ability*.

- Any organization that is ready to embrace innovation must have the *technical ability* to develop new ways of working and new products or services, the *entrepreneurial will* to try out new ideas and take risks, the ability to *learn from experience*, and an understanding of the *needs of users*. They also *pay attention to marketing*, their *development work is undertaken efficiently* and they have a strong *commitment to evolutionary development*.

- US academic Rosabeth Moss Kanter found that the ability of managers to bring about innovatory change relies on their access to *information, resources* and *support*.

- The three main approaches to implementing innovations in organizations are *Mission-oriented, Negotiation* and *Action research*.

Performance checks

Jot down your answers to these questions on *Managing Creativity and Innovation in the Workplace.*

Question 1   Complete these two definitions:

_____ is 'the thinking of novel and appropriate ideas'

_____ is 'the successful implementation of those ideas within an organization'

Question 2   What are the six types of response to innovative products and services:

1

2

3

4

5

6

Question 3   Complete these four stages in the innovation cycle:

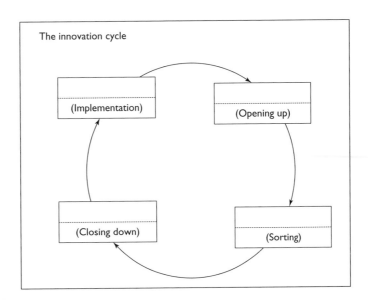

The innovation cycle

(Implementation)

(Opening up)

(Closing down)

(Sorting)

Question 4   List four techniques for generating creative ideas to solve problems or develop new processes, products or services:

1

2

3

4

Question 5   In the Theory of Inventive Problem Solving, what are the four stages in the development of creative solutions to problems?

1

2

3

4

Question 6   What does SCAMPER stand for?

S

C

A

M

P

E

R

Question 7   Explain what is meant by a paradigm.

_____

_____

Question 8   Complete this table showing Altshuller's five levels of inventiveness and the sources of knowledge for each:

Level	Level of inventiveness	Source of knowledge
1	Routine solution, no _____	Personal knowledge
2	Minor improvement, some novelty	_____ _____
3	_____ _____, quite novel	Within the industry
4	New concept, very novel	_____ ___ _____
5	Discovery, _____ ___	'All that is knowable'

Question 9   List the four techniques for judging ideas that come out of the creative process
1
2
3
4

Question 10   Which kind of ability needed for innovation is described by these three statements?

_____	Develop new ways of working and new products or services
_____	Try out new ideas and take risks
_____	Use the experience of developing innovative ways of working, and new products or services (and, in the latter case, taking them to market)

Question 11   According to Bill Coyne, what six characteristics did 3M have to encourage innovation
1
2
3
4
5
6

Question 12   What did Rosabeth Moss Kanter say were needed to enable innovations to be implemented successfully?

_____

_____

_____

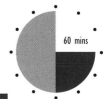

2 Workbook assessment

Read the following case study and then answer the questions that follow. Write your answers on a separate sheet of paper.

Paula manages a large team of customer service agents in a call centre of an insurance company. Their role is to deal with customers calling up to make claims on their car and household policies. At the moment agents take details from customers and then send out claim forms for customers to check and sign. Once these are received back they are checked again, and allocated to the regional claims offices where they are then allocated to an individual claims adjuster.

In theory this whole process should take about five days, but it often takes two or three weeks, and it then takes up to six months to settle the claims. This is causing a lot of dissatisfaction amongst customers.

Paula persuades her manager to let her examine how the process and the service to customers could be improved. She manages to get two claims adjusters and an administrator from one of the regional offices to join some members of her team in a group to develop some creative ideas.

The group brainstorms the problems and they come up with a wide range of possible ways of addressing the problem. Some of these would involve very significant and innovative changes in the organization; others are less innovative. Paula is now unsure what to do next with all these ideas.

Advise Paula on:

1   The next steps she needs to take with all her creative ideas.

2   How she can judge how ready the organization is to accept the more innovative changes.

3   The importance of having information, support and resources to ensure the innovation is implemented successfully.

3 Work-based assignment

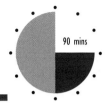

90 mins

The time guide for this assignment gives you an approximate idea of how long it is likely to take you to write up your findings. You will find you need to spend some additional time gathering information, perhaps talking to colleagues and thinking about the assignment. The result of your efforts should be presented on separate sheets of paper.

Your written response to this assignment may provide the basis of appropriate evidence for your S/NVQ portfolio.

What you have to do

Identify an issue within your area of responsibility where your organization would benefit from innovation. This could be a quality problem or a possible product or service development to meet actual or potential customer needs.

Discuss the issue with your manager and agree what constraints may exist on the limits of innovation.

Lead a group through a creative ideas generation process to develop a range of ideas. Sort these and evaluate them (close down) to decide which ones are viable, and select the most appropriate ideas, based on your assessment of the level of innovation that the organization is able to accept.

Prepare a plan to put the innovation into place, taking account of the characteristics needed for successful implementation.

Reflect and review

1 Reflect and review

Now that you have completed your work on *Managing Creativity and Innovation in the Workplace*, let us review each of our unit objectives.

The first objective was:

■ Distinguish between creativity and innovation

We have used definitions of creativity and innovation that make it clear that innovation depends on creativity. We have also emphasized that everyone has the ability to be creative, given the opportunity, and that a key part of any managers' role is to take advantage of the creative ability of the people they lead.

Can you readily distinguish between the two ideas?

_____

_____

Do you trust in the people you lead to develop creative ideas, given the right opportunity?

_____

_____

The next objective was:

■ Recognize the increasing importance of creativity and innovation in organizational success

We have seen how innovative products and services, and ways of working, have become far more prevalent and that people are far more ready to accept innovation than in the past. We have also seen how hard it is to recognize all the opportunities to be innovative, but all organizations need to have a commitment to creativity and innovation and have systems in place to develop their own creative ideas, and also seek out creativity and innovation from other sources.

How willing are you to try out innovative products and services? Which of the six categories we looked at best describes you?

_____

_____

Does your organization actively encourage and seek out creative ideas and innovative processes, products and services?

_____

_____

The next two objectives were:

- Appreciate some of the different techniques that can help you to lead people through a creative ideas generation process
- Select an appropriate creative approach to developing innovations in your organization

We looked at several different techniques, four of them in some detail. Although they may look demanding, once you try them you will find they are quite straightforward to use.

Do you feel confident to use any of the different techniques for creative ideas generation?

_____

_____

What are you going to do to try any of them out?

_____

_____

The final objective was:

- Implement innovative ideas in your organization

It's one thing to develop creative ideas for new processes, products or services, it's another to put them into practice. We looked at what it takes for an organization to be open to innovative ideas and what you as manager need if you are to be able to do so effectively.

How receptive is your organization to innovation? What characteristics does it have that cause you to make that judgement?

_____

_____

Do you believe that you will be able to implement innovative ideas in your organization?

_____

_____

2 Action plan

Use this plan to further develop for yourself a course of action you want to take. Make a note in the left-hand column of the issues or problems you want to tackle, and then decide what you intend to do, and make a note in Column 2.

The resources you need might include time, materials, information or money. You may need to negotiate for some of them, but they could be something easily acquired, like half an hour of somebody's time, or a chapter of a book. Put whatever you need in Column 3. No plan means anything without a timescale, so put a realistic target completion date in Column 4.

Finally, describe the outcome you want to achieve as a result of this plan, whether it is for your own benefit or advancement, or a more efficient way of doing things.

Desired outcomes				
	1 Issues	2 Action	3 Resources	4 Target completion
Actual outcomes				

3 Extensions

Extension 1	Book	*Systematic Innovation: Introduction to the Theory of Inventive Problem Solving (TRIZ)*
	Authors	John Terninko, Alla Zusman, Boris Zlotin
	Publisher	St Lucie Press (1998)

Extension 2	Book	*Creative Problem Solving for Managers: Developing Skills for Decision Making and Innovation*
	Author	Tony Proctor
	Publisher	Routledge (2005)

4 Answers to self-assessment questions

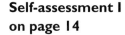

Self-assessment 1 on page 14

1 Creativity is 'the thinking of novel and appropriate ideas' whereas innovation is 'the successful implementation of those ideas within an organization.'

2 The innovation gap.

3 Innovators, Early Adopters, Early Majorities, Late Majorities, Late Adopters and Laggards.

Reflect and review

**Self-assessment 2
on pages 35–7**

1

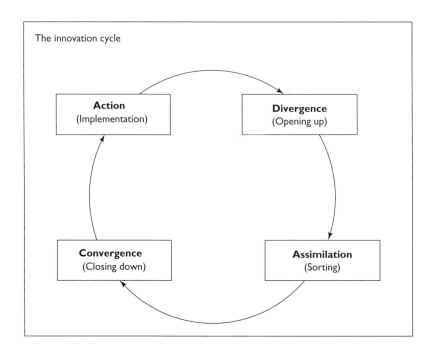

The innovation cycle

Action
(Implementation)

Divergence
(Opening up)

Convergence
(Closing down)

Assimilation
(Sorting)

2   The rules of brainstorming are as follows:

- Make sure the purpose is clear and understood.

- Control the group, make sure everyone takes part and nobody dominates.

- Every idea is allowed and written up for all to see.

- Build on the ideas of others, don't discuss or object to them.

3   Two variants on brainstorming are Nominal Group Technique and Trigger Sessions.

4   TRIZ stands for Theory of Inventive Problem Solving.

5   The five inventive principles mean:

1 *Segmentation* – divide a product into sections that fit together.

2 *Extraction* – remove something that is causing a problem.

3 *Local quality* – introduce variations to meet specific requirements of the environment.

4 *Asymmetry* – make symmetrical objects asymmetric.

5 *Combining* – link together items that need to work together.

6   The four stages in the TRIZ problem-solving process are:

- State the problem

- Look for an analogous standard problem

- Explore the solution to this analogous problem

- Adapt this solution to your own problem.

7   Just 1% of solutions to problems involved a radically new discovery

8   SCAMPER stands for:

■ Substitute (components, materials, people or processes).

■ Combine (things or activities together).

■ Adapt (or change an activity or object).

■ Modify (something, making it bigger or smaller, change its shape or its features).

■ Put (something to another use).

■ Eliminate (something by removing components of stages in a process, simplify things and reduce them to their core functionality).

■ Reverse (something, turning inside out or upside down, or ask how you would do the reverse of what you want to do, to suggest how to do it better).

9   Synectics is based on bringing together contradictory or very different ideas in order to generate a creative solution to a problem.

10   Two other techniques similar to synectics are Lateral thinking and Random juxtaposition.

Self-assessment 3   1

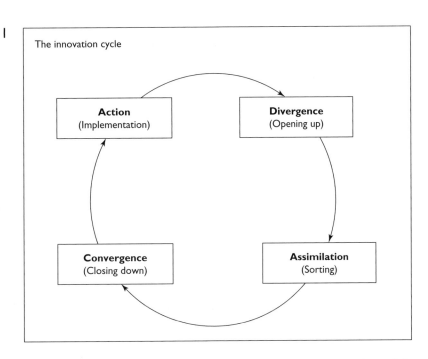

The innovation cycle

2   What are the two questions you should ask to decide on the viability of creative ideas?

1 Would they work?

2 Can this organization make them work?

3 Thomas Kuhn claled the dominant mindset that shapes how scientists respond to new ideas, a paradigm

4 Four techniques to judge the ideas from the creative ideas process:

- Hurdles

- Ranking

- Weighting

- Instinct

5 The two types of technical innovation identified by CEST were:

- evolutionary innovation

- revolutionary innovation

6 The three core competences required for innovation are:

1 technological – the ability to develop new ways of working and new products or services;

2 entrepreneurial – the willingness to try out new ideas and take risks; and

3 learning – the ability to learn from the innovative experience

7 Any organization that is ready to embrace *innovation* must have the *technical* ability to develop new ways of working and new products or services, the *entrepreneurial* will to try out new ideas and take risks, the ability to *learn* from experience, and an understanding of the needs of *users*. They also pay attention to *marketing*, their development work is undertaken *efficiently* and they have a strong commitment to evolutionary *development*.

8 According to Rosabeth Moss Kanter, the power to bring about innovatory change relies on:

- Information

- Resources

- Support

9 The three main approaches to implementing innovations in organizations are:

- Mission-oriented

- Negotiaiton

- Action research

5 Answers to activities

Activity 17

	Our order	Our reasons
1.	Financial Services Authority must be prepared to licence us to offer it.	If they can't be licensed then there is no point in continuing with the idea.
2.	Customers must think us a suitable source.	It is hard – and expensive – to change customer opinions.
3.	No other organizations dominate the market.	If there is a dominant supplier then they will be facing a hard battle to get established.
4.	We must already have the skills to offer it.	Useful but not essential – skills can be learned or staff recruited.
5.	Must be able to be supplied via the Internet.	Again, this is useful and, in the long run, may be essential, but the Internet only accounts for a fraction of the market, even if it's growing, and some customers are still not that keen on using it.

You may have put some of these in different orders – 2 and 3 could be swapped, as can 4 and 5, but the general order reflects increasingly demanding hurdles that really sort out the ideas.

Activity 18

Our rank order

1 Offer to deliver to workplaces.

2 Ask for a neighbour's name and address as an alternative delivery address.

3 Use a tamper-proof container that can be locked to the letterbox with a release code that can be sent by text when the person requests it.

4 Deliver in the evenings and weekends.

5 Use local delivery points, such as post offices, for people to collect their items in their own time.

You may have come up with something different, but see how your answers compare with ours and think about why they may differ.

Activity 19

Characteristics	Our weights for each
Financial Services Authority must be prepared to licence us to offer it	5
We must already have the skills to offer it	1
Customers must think us a suitable source	4
Must be able to be supplied via the Internet	2
No other organizations dominate the market	4

You may have come up with something different, but see how your answers compare with ours and think about why they may differ.

⬤ 6 Answers to the quick quiz

Answer 1 Complete these two definitions:
CREATIVITY is 'the thinking of novel and appropriate ideas' INNOVATION is 'the successful implementation of those ideas within an organization.'

Answer 2 INNOVATORS, EARLY ADOPTERS, EARLY MAJORITIES, LATE MAJORITIES, LATE ADOPTERS and LAGGARDS.

Answer 3

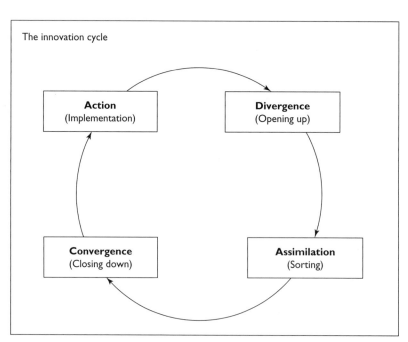

The innovation cycle

Action (Implementation) → Divergence (Opening up) → Assimilation (Sorting) → Convergence (Closing down) → Action (Implementation)

Answer 4   Four from: BRAINSTORMING, TRIZ, SCAMPER, SYNECTICS, NOMINAL GROUP TECHNIQUE, TRIGGER SESSIONS, LATERAL THINKING or RANDOM JUXTAPOSITION.

Answer 5   The four stages in the TRIZ approach to solving problems are: STATE THE PROBLEM, LOOK FOR AN ANALOGOUS STANDARD PROBLEM, EXPLORE THE SOLUTION TO THIS ANALOGOUS PROBLEM and ADAPT THIS SOLUTION TO YOUR OWN PROBLEM.

Answer 6   SUBSTITUTE, COMBINE, ADAPT, MODIFY, PUT, ELIMINATE, REVERSE.

Answer 7   Paradigms are accepted ways of thinking and doing things, the explanation that is broadly accepted as the right one in any scientific community.

Answer 8

Level	Level of inventiveness	Source of knowledge
1	Routine solution, no NOVELTY	Personal knowledge
2	Minor improvement, some novelty	WITHIN ORGANIZATION
3	MAJOR IMPROVEMENT, quite novel	Within the industry
4	New concept, very novel	OUTSIDE THE INDUSTRY
5	Discovery, RADICALLY NEW	'All that is knowable'

Answer 9   The four techniques for judging ideas that come out of the creative process are HURDLES, RANKING, WEIGHTING and INSTINCT.

Answer 10   The innovation described by the three statements are:

1 TECHNOLOGICAL – the ability to develop new ways of working and new products or services.
2 ENTREPRENEURIAL – the willingness to try out new ideas and take risks.
3 LEARNING – the ability to learn from the experience of developing innovative ways of working, and new products or services (and, in the latter case, taking them to market).

Answer 11   3M's six characteristics claimed to encourage innovation:

1 Vision
2 Foresight
3 Stretch goals
4 Empowerment
5 Communication
6 Rewards and recognition

Answer 12 Rosabeth Moss Kanter said that for innovations to be implemented success-fully managers needed:

- Information
- Resources
- Support

7 Certificate

Completion of this certificate by an authorized person shows that you have worked through all the parts of this workbook and satisfactorily completed the assessments. The certificate provides a record of what you have done that may be used for exemptions or as evidence of prior learning against other nationally certificated qualifications.

superseries

Managing Creativity and Innovation in the Workplace

....

has satisfactorily completed this workbook

Name of signatory ....

Position ....

Signature ....

Date ....

Official stamp

Pergamon
Flexible
Learning

Fifth Edition

superseries

FIFTH EDITION

Workbooks in the series:

Achieving Objectives Through Time Management	978-0-08-046415-2
Building the Team	978-0-08-046412-1
Coaching and Training your Work Team	978-0-08-046418-3
Communicating One-to-One at Work	978-0-08-046438-1
Developing Yourself and Others	978-0-08-046414-5
Effective Meetings for Managers	978-0-08-046439-8
Giving Briefings and Making Presentations in the Workplace	978-0-08-046436-7
Influencing Others at Work	978-0-08-046435-0
Introduction to Leadership	978-0-08-046411-4
Managing Conflict in the Workplace	978-0-08-046416-9
Managing Creativity and Innovation in the Workplace	978-0-08-046441-1
Managing Customer Service	978-0-08-046419-0
Managing Health and Safety at Work	978-0-08-046426-8
Managing Performance	978-0-08-046429-9
Managing Projects	978-0-08-046425-1
Managing Stress in the Workplace	978-0-08-046417-6
Managing the Effective Use of Equipment	978-0-08-046432-9
Managing the Efficient Use of Materials	978-0-08-046431-2
Managing the Employment Relationship	978-0-08-046443-5
Marketing for Managers	978-0-08-046974-4
Motivating to Perform in the Workplace	978-0-08-046413-8
Obtaining Information for Effective Management	978-0-08-046434-3
Organizing and Delegating	978-0-08-046422-0
Planning Change in the Workplace	978-0-08-046444-2
Planning to Work Efficiently	978-0-08-046421-3
Providing Quality to Customers	978-0-08-046420-6
Recruiting, Selecting and Inducting New Staff in the Workplace	978-0-08-046442-8
Solving Problems and Making Decisions	978-0-08-046423-7
Understanding Change in the Workplace	978-0-08-046424-4
Understanding Culture and Ethics in Organizations	978-0-08-046428-2
Understanding Organizations in their Context	978-0-08-046427-5
Understanding the Communication Process in the Workplace	978-0-08-046433-6
Understanding Workplace Information Systems	978-0-08-046440-4
Working with Costs and Budgets	978-0-08-046430-5
Writing for Business	978-0-08-046437-4

For prices and availability please telephone our order helpline
or email

+44 (0) 1865 474010

directorders@elsevier.com